The Executive's Guide to Buying Commercial Property

How to Avoid Common Pitfalls When Buying a Building

By Alex Ruggieri, CRE, CCIM, SEC, CIPS, MBA
and
Noah Ruggieri, CIPS, MBA

Joe,

Thank you for your friendship and support. You are and outstanding example to all in our industry!

The Executive's Guide to Buying Commercial Property
How to Avoid Common Pitfalls When Buying a Building
by Alex Ruggieri and Noah Ruggieri
Copyright © 2018 Alex Ruggieri
Published by SkillBites LLC
www.SkillBites.net
All rights reserved.

This title is available at discount when purchased in bulk.
Email info@skillbites.net or call 855-SKILLBITES with inquiry.

DISCLAIMER AND LEGAL NOTICES
While the publisher and authors have used their best efforts in preparing this book, they make no representations or warranties with respect to the accuracy or completeness of the contents of this book. The advice and strategies contained herein may not be suitable for your situation. You should consult a professional where appropriate. Neither the publisher nor the authors shall be liable for any loss of profit or any other commercial damages, including but not limited to special, incidental, consequential, or other damages. The purchaser or reader of this publication assumes responsibility for the use of these materials and information. Adherence to all applicable laws and regulations, both advertising and all other aspects of doing business in the United States or any other jurisdiction, is the sole responsibility of the purchaser or reader.

ISBN-10: 1-942489-62-5
ISBN-13: 978-1-942489-62-7

Praise for The Executive's Guide to Buying Commercial Property

"A quick read, short and to the point. A must-read for anyone entering the commercial real estate world!"

—Paul Tatman
Real Estate Entrepreneur

"Sensible, practical advice...a comprehensive account on how to approach the purchase of commercial real estate."

—Albert M. Berriz
Chief Executive Officer, Co-Owner, and Managing Member
McKinley, Inc.

"As the most respected real estate specialists in the industry, Counselors are known for innovation and problem solving. As a CRE, Ruggieri has embodied that tradition with a well written guidebook for the executive."

—Joseph G. Nahas, Jr., CRE, FRICS
Senior Vice President, Institutional Marketing and Investor Relations
Equus Capital Partners, LTD
2018 Chair, Board of Directors of the Counselors of Real Estate

"Alex Ruggieri's in-depth real estate experience truly makes him a 'realtor's realtor' who not only understands the logistical aspects of a deal but more importantly the human component as well."

—Dan Wagner
Senior Vice President of Government Relations
The Inland Real Estate Group, LLC

"This insightful and extremely helpful book could have a profound effect on your business. The practical tips provide a clear and crisp approach to seemingly complex real estate investing. It is a must-read before you purchase your next building!"

—J.M. Jim Schultz
Chairman/CEO
Open Prairie Private Equity Group

"Alex Ruggieri has provided answers to the exact issues faced by most executives, both new and seasoned, when acquiring commercial real estate. He addresses how to structure the acquisition and shares excellent hands-on examples. All in clear and readable prose! A must-read if you are in the market."

—Judith A. Hermanson, PhD
President & CEO
IHC Global

"Alex is a commercial practitioner with a national profile, yet he has managed to condense his considerable know-how into a precise guidebook that executives can count on to help them avoid the faux pas most make in a real estate purchase."

—Gene Trowbridge, Esq. CCIM, CDEI
Trowbridge Sidoti LLP

"If you are in the position of acquiring property for your business, I strongly urge you to read *The Executive's Guide to Real Estate* before you begin. It could not only help you avoid costly common mistakes, but could save you thousands of dollars in the process."

—Mike Hedge
Chief Executive Officer and President
Birkey's Farm Store, Inc.

"I wish this book had been around when I bought my first business property in 2001. The appendix 'Acquisition of Real Estate—Comprehensive Due Diligence Checklist' is indeed a comprehensive guide that I will use in the future."

—Dr. David Fletcher, MD, MPH, FACOEM
Owner
Safeworks Illinois

"Owning our commercial real estate has been one of the best things we have done for our business. It now allows us more options financially. Banks always like the fact that we own our buildings. If you have the chance to buy a building for your business, by all means, do it! But read Alex's book before you buy."

—Kevin Applebee
CEO
Flooring Surfaces Inc.

"Alex has established himself on a national level as one of the leading commercial practitioners in our industry today. In *The Executive's Guide to Buying Commercial Real Estate*, he shares his experience in a manner that is easy to understand and profit from."

—Kevin Maggiacomo
President & CEO
SVN International, Corp.

"Buy the book before the building. Avoid the pitfalls of commercial property acquisition by making sure your due diligence includes reading *The Executive's Guide to Buying Commercial Property*."

—Dan Hamelberg
Real Estate Developer and Founder of University Group

"In his profession, Alex stands as tall as they get. In a field where there are a lot of imitators and poseurs, he walks with honesty and integrity. If you have a real estate issue, call Alex. If you can't, at a minimum read the book!"

—Don Bartos
CEO
Dimond Bros. Insurance

"Alex has provided a simple, straightforward roadmap to the sometimes daunting process of acquiring or developing commercial real estate, even covering matters that some experts might overlook or forget. I would keep this on my desk (or in my pocket) as a handy guide for when things, inevitably, go haywire."

—Peter C. Burley, CRE FRICS
Real Estate Market and Economics Research and Strategy Development

"Commercial real estate is one of the best ways to generate wealth, but it can also get you into trouble if you don't know what you're doing. In this practical and easy-to-follow guide, Alex Ruggieri does an outstanding job of showing busy executives exactly how they can profit from today's lucrative but sometimes uncertain real estate market."

—Jeff Beals
Author, Speaker, and Executive Consultant

"Alex Ruggieri's counsel in commercial real estate is highly regarded and coveted, and having it in book form is a must for anyone buying a building. Whether you're buying your first property or adding to a portfolio, this book is a must-read."

—Janet Branton, CAE, CIPS
Senior Vice President of Commercial, Global, and Affiliate Services
National Association of REALTORS®

"Alex is passionate about helping people grow their businesses regardless of the size of their company. His real estate expertise is condensed into this book. I would definitely want him on my team!"

—Chris Saunders
President
Green Street Realty

"Alex Ruggieri knows what to look for (and what not do) when buying a building. He has outlined straightforward, common-sense strategies into an invaluable guide for executives and business owners."

—Gary Harvey
CFO
AF Holdings

"I have seen firsthand the ability and knowledge of Alex Ruggeri in the real estate arena. The advice contained in *The Executive's Guide to Buying Commercial Property* is undeniably helpful. If you have to buy or build, I urge you to read this book!"

—Mike Cohan
President
AF Holdings

Table of Contents

Acknowledgments 1

Dedication 3

Introduction 5

Chapter One 7

Chapter Two 15

Chapter Three 25

Chapter Four 35

Chapter Five 43

Resources 55

About the Authors 57

Appendix 59

    Exhibit A 87

    Exhibit B 94

    Exhibit C 97

Acknowledgments

I would like to acknowledge my beautiful wife Sylvia for all her support over the last forty-five-plus years. She more than any other has been there when I needed support. I also want to thank all the customers and clients who have supported me over the years by trusting me to represent them in one of the most important business decisions a company has to make: buying a building.

I would like to thank my friend and mentor Paul Tatman who over the years, while being a client, has also taken the time to counsel me and point me in the right direction when needed.

Judy Weintraub of SkillBites has been an invaluable guide along the path of producing this volume. Her dedication, along with a lot of help from Mike Valentino, has made what first seemed like an almost impossible task not only achievable but a lot of fun as well.

Finally, no acknowledgement would be complete without thanking my team, particularly my son Noah Ruggieri and my daughter-in-law Jessica Ruggieri, for without their help, none of my work would be possible.

Dedication

This book is dedicated to you, the executive whose responsibility includes having to tackle the daunting task of buying or building a commercial property for your business. If one idea saves you time, money or from making a costly mistake, it will all have been worth the effort.

Introduction

Y ou've just learned that you are to be the go-to guy for the acquisition of your company's new building. You see no real challenge. After all, you've managed a few projects in the past and maybe you've even bought a few homes. This should be in your wheelhouse.

Well...there might be far more to consider than you may have realized. You may be a whiz when it comes to the products or services of your industry, but imagine, for example, if someone asked you to design a website for the first time. With no real experience, imagine the problems you could face when buying a building for your company. These can involve everything from zoning issues to financial complications to community opposition to the project. What can you do? The answer is simple. Arm yourself with the facts. This guide is for executives who understand their own business inside and out, but could benefit greatly from solid advice and guidance when it comes to commercial real estate.

The authors of this book have over 50 years combined in commercial real estate, primarily handling larger transactions in the multimillions of dollars, and have sold over $500 Million in property (including $55 Million just this past year). Besides buying and selling buildings, they also have immense experience in commercial building projects.

They have won national sales awards numerous times, and are leaders in their industry associations, both at the national level and state level. Both authors are also Certified International Property Specialists, a select group of commercial brokers with this designation whose purpose is to work across international borders with buyers and sellers to complete real estate transactions. They have seen practically every problem that can come up in a commercial real estate transaction. Their aim with this book is to help companies avoid the typical pitfalls that inexperienced executives encounter when buying a building for the first time.

Chapter One

Real estate investing, even on a very small scale, remains a tried and true means of building an individual's cash flow and wealth.

–Robert Kiyosaki

Why Buy Your Building?

For most prospective building owners, the tendency, of course, is to oversimplify things. How complicated can buying a building be? Isn't it fairly similar to buying residential property? That kind of thinking can sink even a seasoned executive into financial quicksand. The process is not nearly as straightforward as one may assume, even for experienced businesspeople filled with confidence in their ability to navigate all things financial.

For example, have you or anyone on the staff ever dealt with city government in relation to building or acquiring a building in their neighborhood for a company in your line of business? Are you or anyone on the staff up-to-date on all city ordinances and pitfalls in acquiring or building a new building?

Over my many decades as a commercial real estate broker, I have seen countless examples of business owners either taking the do-it-yourself route or assigning the job to someone in the company who is not qualified for the task.

These are monumental blunders they ultimately regret. The buying process is loaded with pitfalls and common mistakes—but thankfully, they are all avoidable.

Whether you are launching a new business or you need new space for expansion, you will find this easy-to-follow guide indispensable over the long term. Real estate is an important piece of the puzzle when it comes to the health of any company. The choices that you make now will have serious repercussions—good or bad—for many years to come.

Before looking at the common problems a business owner might encounter in seeking to buy a building and how to overcome those issues, it might help to briefly review the benefits of owning versus leasing/renting the property for your business.

The primary reason to own the building that houses your business is that ownership lets you take control of your own destiny. You no longer have to worry about the landlord raising your rent or pushing you out of the property when you aren't ready to relocate. You don't have to ask permission to make improvements to the space or the grounds. There are no limitations on how you manage signage, and you can respond to the need to expand or revise the space your business uses in your own way and on your own timetable.

An important aspect of controlling your destiny—and that of your business—is for all the rights of ownership to be in your favor. No one is telling you what to do or how to do it, which is especially important when your business is growing or adapting to changes in the marketplace.

The financial aspect of ownership is another key factor to keep in mind. I have seen the bulk of a building owner's net worth come from owning the building that is home to a business, rather than from the business itself. This is not always the case, of course, but, unlike the unpredictable winds of business, real estate has over the years demonstrated an uncanny ability to inevitably increase in value. While you are immersed in the day-to-day routine of running the business, your equity in the property is quietly building in the background, almost like a silent savings account.

As the owner of the building, you also reap the benefits of other major advantages, such as interest and deductions for various other ownership-related expenses.

Here's a great example of the potential value of owning your building.

Stanley Kaplan sold his renowned test-preparation company to Westinghouse for $50 million. I met him when he was visiting his various campuses around the country and I was in the Executive MBA program at the University of Illinois in Champaign.

"You must be ecstatic about the sale," I said to him. He said yes, it was a wonderful thing—but he regretted never having owned any real estate affiliated with his company.

"I had so many schools—around 125—on campuses all over the country, and I had opportunities to buy," he told me. "Every time an opportunity came up, I would go to my accountant, and every time, my accountant would say, 'Stanley, you're in the education business, not the real estate business.' One was a building in California for sale for $6 million. That building just sold for *$100 million*. Imagine how much money I would have made if I had owned the buildings where I had schools when I was ready to sell the business!"

I have seen other instances in which a business wasn't worth much in and of itself, but *the building it was in* was worth $100 million.

The lesson here is that real estate in business is a distinct and potentially valuable part of the investment. One part of the value of your business is the business itself, and the other part is the real estate.

Here are the nuts and bolts of the situation.

From a purely financial point of view, if you rent your business space, every rental check you pay is money that you will never see again. If you own the property, every payment on your mortgage lowers your total mortgage, thus can be considered money in the bank. This is a big difference from money out the window.

As great as that is, it is not the end of the money advantage story. Commercial real estate (just like any asset you use to earn an income) can be depreciated. What does this mean? Say you depreciate your building over a twenty-year period. If the building cost $400,000, you can take a tax deduction of $20,000 per year on your taxes. A considerable sum and a great savings. Look at what this adds up to over twenty years!

You can also depreciate other parts of your plant and equipment, for example, any machinery you use to make your product and earn money as well as any ancillary equipment such as air conditioners. I know of a case where the owner of a building had five air conditioning units on the roof and didn't realize he could depreciate them until a segregation engineer gave him this info. The units were worth over $300,000. A nice little write-off over a five-year period.

You can, of course, also deduct your mortgage interest and real estate taxes for the building. A good tax accountant can no doubt find additional building-related expenses that can be deducted.

Then there's another interesting advantage: Appreciation. This is the amount of money by which your building's value in the marketplace increases each year. Think of what a tidy amount this can come to in twenty years, giving you a valuable asset that can be leveraged to your advantage in a number of ways. Owning the building, therefore, offers a powerful hedge against inflation.

Are there any negatives on this rosy picture? Sure. But they are negligible, all things considered. We will go into that later.

There are other advantages to building ownership that may not be so readily apparent. First and foremost: the lack of landlord disputes. Because every business is a unique operation, and because one of the fundamentals of business is to grow and expand, you need as much freedom as possible. Let's say you decide that by knocking out a wall, you can make your operation more efficient and more profitable. Basically, all you need is a weekend, a sledgehammer, and a dustpan—but without permission, you can't do it. So, you go to the landlord with your idea and your request to knock out a wall. Why would the landlord refuse? A better question might be, why not? Think about it. What's in it for him? Nothing, unless he charges you more rent for the privilege of the renovation. As a renter, you can't even beautify your front entrance without the approval of the landlord. He has absolutely no obligation to help you. He has a lease that you're bound to. Depending on the terms of your lease, you may literally need permission to do so much as plant flowers at your entryway.

Now, you might have a great landlord, and he might agree to the things you need for your business, but remember: a landlord is a businessperson too, with an eye out for profit—or extra profit. Your destiny, then, is not in your own hands. You are bound by the landlord's whims, needs, and interests.

Let's say, for example, you need an extension on your lease. He could say "sure." Or he can say, well, that hinders me, I only do twelve-month leases. The end result is usually something like, "I can do it but I will have to go up on your rent."

You protest, "I have a lease."

The landlord counters with, "No, your lease is up, remember, you need an extension on your lease; in effect, a new lease."

He has you. And it can be costly.

Another example. Let's say you are running a daycare, a business that is highly regulated by state government. We all know that legislatures are always coming up with new rules and regulations, so let's say they decide you can't have any doors in the facility without windows. You have twelve doors that need to be replaced. Again, you need the landlord's approval. So much for controlling your own destiny!

You can see how needs for changes in the physical plant can arise in any growing business that may not be easy to effect as a renter, thus limiting your potential and growth.

For these and numerous other reasons, it makes sense for many business owners to buy their commercial property. Of course, if you need to relocate for some reason, you can't move without having to sell that building, while renting means more flexibility in that area. However, being able to make such a move may not be as difficult as it seems. A well-maintained building in a good location—that's right, the real estate mantra of "location, location, location"—is likely to sell fairly easily.

Chapter Two

Good things do not come easy. The road is lined with pitfalls.

–Desi Arnaz

Pitfalls and Problems—Common Misconceptions, Errors, and Issues

One of the biggest mistakes that a prospective owner makes when ready to buy a building for a business is to do it on their own, or assign the task to the wrong person—usually someone in management; perhaps the company's chief financial officer or accountant.

This doesn't work for a number of reasons. First and foremost, neither the owner nor that manager is a real estate expert. No matter how savvy or skilled in their business roles, neither one is likely to see far enough beyond short-term planning to envision how the business might grow to need more space in the future. Neither is likely to understand the many ways a commercial real estate process can work—or not work—to the advantage of the business and its owner. Neither is objective enough to see the purchase clearly and without limitations. Neither is an expert in commercial real estate, and such an expert is what you need.

Assigning oneself or a staffer to the process of buying a building is a major issue because it also can damage the current day-to-day strength of the operation. It takes that person away from his or her core responsibilities and competencies; from doing what he or she needs to do for the best interests of the company and making the best use of those competencies; and from what they are there to do.

Buying real estate is a complex process, even more so for a business than for a residence. It's like a Rubik's Cube—for the process to work, all the pieces have to move around until they fit together in a neat, almost geometrical pattern.

Just as you wouldn't hire a divorce attorney to handle patent proceedings, you shouldn't hire a residential real estate professional for this commercial process. The right adviser is critical to success.

Among the classic pitfalls is for the business owner to indulge in a building purchase and design that is so individualistic and idiosyncratic that no one else will ever want that property in the future. And you do have to keep the future in mind: One day, you will want to hand off or sell the business and that building, so it has to work not just for your business today and tomorrow, but for someone else's business further down the line.

For example, I had a good friend who wanted to build a corporate headquarters for his thriving business and didn't ask anyone anything in the process of doing so. He built a monument to himself that was specific only to his business and his personality, and couldn't be adapted for other uses. When he later put the building up for sale, he had no takers. The price was too high, in large part because he was thinking in terms of what he put into it rather than what the market would bear, and the building was far too ornate for anyone else to envision it as a business setting—gold faucets, imported tile in the entryway, copper exterior elements, inflexible floor plans, and more. He never did sell that building.

Here's another example from my own experience. Two college girls formed a partnership and went into the catering business. They were talented cooks and so their business grew rapidly; soon they were in need of a building to accommodate their expansion. They couldn't find the kind of building they needed, so they decided to buy a piece of farmland and build their own. They found a good place outside of town that even had a farmhouse they could rent for income on the property.

Things were looking good for the girls. Then came the first problem: they learned that the land was not zoned for business. Agriculture yes, but not the catering business. Now what? They had an expensive piece of property on their hands that was of no use to them.

They had an attorney file to rezone the land, and after many (profitless) months, they acquired the proper zoning. An expensive lesson, and one that could easily have been averted had they asked the question: Is the property zoned for business? If they learned that it was not, they could have made the purchase contingent upon acquiring the proper zoning. But they didn't. Let's face it, business is tough enough without making rookie mistakes like this.

Short-term thinking is another potential pitfall in the buying process. It pays to think of the future of the business when making such an important purchase. A building that is big enough and configured appropriately for today's version of your company is not enough. When you make this investment, you need to think in terms of what the business might need not just this and next year, but five years down the road. Keeping success in mind, that means your business is likely to expand and need more, or differently configured, space. Because both a building purchase and a relocation are expensive propositions, you want to make such a purchase with the goal of not needing to go through that again anytime soon.

When you decide to buy a building, think of what you will do with it when your business is successful enough to need to expand again, or once you're ready to sell and retire. Keep the questions "How can this property serve us in the future?" and "Who is the next logical owner?" in mind when you purchase, design, and accessorize. That's just one of countless potential issues that a competent professional can advise you about before you become the owner of that building.

To help prevent some of these problems before they take root, it's a good idea to have a conversation with an appraiser ahead of time. Talking to other building owners in the area is also recommended. You might, for example, find out that the buildings on your street were just assessed to pay for a new traffic signal on the corner!

Of course, the way you structure your transaction is critical, too. I remember an instance when we wanted to build a subdivision, so we bought some land for the project. As part of the process, we needed to have approval from the city council for what we wanted to build, and in this case people in the neighborhood were demanding all sorts of things. They wanted a double sidewalk, erosion control, all kinds of extras that added costs to the existing expense. If you spend too much, obviously, there is no profit in the end.

A lot of what these other parties will ask for in such situations basically constitute a "wish list." They are trying to spend other people's money. We want "hot and cold running maids," as the old joke goes. That is why it is so important to structure your contract so that it gives you an option to purchase AFTER your due diligence is satisfied. That way, you can walk away if you don't get what you need. We said, "Here is what we'll do; here is what our team's engineer says is all that is needed. Our proposal seems reasonable to us and if we don't get it, we will have no choice but to walk away." Guess what? Everybody backed off. We wanted to build this, so we were willing to compromise. We could have boxed ourselves in. If we had gone ahead and bought the property before settling these issues, it would have been a very big risk. I call it a whistle clause. Somebody blows a whistle and says, "Hey, wait a second!"

After the purchase, you should gather all the records. If you had a survey done, keep a copy of that survey with the deeds, floor plan, fire marshal evacuation report, etc. Go ahead and create a digital file as well. Ten years from now, you're going to need these records if you want to sell. It would be hard to gather all that information again after a decade has passed, so it is sure to come in handy.

NIMBY

Another common problem you need to be aware of is called NIMBY: *Not In My Backyard.* That is one of the many reasons why it is always so crucial to know as much as possible about the area where you want to buy or build property. What is the predominant local socioeconomic status; what are the residents' values, politics, etc.? Get a feel for these things by talking to people on the city council and others involved with regulatory issues, such as the water authority people. You need to be certain there are not any kind of serious NIMBY objections looming just over the horizon.

The reality is that there can come a point where the objections mount so high that ultimately you decide against the project. If you find you have neighborhood opposition, try to meet with them and talk away from public meetings or council meetings. Sit down with them and have a cup of coffee.

We did a subdivision one time, and we arranged to meet at one of the members' homes. It is amazing how few real estate developers think of that. If you meet with them and they see that you are a reasonable person, you don't have horns, and are not trying to destroy their neighborhood but are trying to improve things—that goes a long way to taking the edge off. They see you as a real person.

Solutions might be easier than you had realized. Maybe all they want is some extra landscaping so that they won't have to stare at your warehouse. Sometimes this is all it takes. You probably were going to do that anyway. There may be a cost-effective solution. Show them you value their concerns. Listen, and see if there's a way you can accommodate them within reason. Again, it's important that you are working with an option so you can walk away if necessary.

Also keep in mind that if you are making an addition or remodeling, the next thing you know you will be making alterations or changes that need approval on the city, administrative, or council level. You need to realize that these entities typically comprise volunteers or political appointees.

I remember one project where the planning board ruled against the zoning change we wanted. Our plan was to put a CVS on a plot occupied by an old church and a bunch of 1960s-era houses. The planning board didn't want to do that. They said that they would recommend zoning it for apartments. However, we had a contract with CVS, so what do you do, given such circumstances? First, keep in mind that the city council doesn't always have to do what the planning board recommends. The planning board's function is to be the first line of analysis and recommendation, but they are not the ultimate authority. The powers that be rest with the city council.

We had a one-on-one meeting with the concerned individuals, during which we showed them how it would increase taxes—a lot. We agreed to put in some street repairs, $150,000 worth. They all said they would support it even though it was not recommended, and the city council approved it. This is an example of why you must be aware of the process. Just because you get one or two noes doesn't mean you can't get it done. It is also good advice to stick within the areas you know. That's where it becomes important to hire a good law firm and broker who are well connected locally.

Not Finding the Right Building

This, of course, is what it all boils down to in this business. Obviously, this is where your team is going to come into play. If you have a good commercial real estate broker, they can be the point person who tells you all that you need to know about the market where you have an interest. I recommend you find one broker you can work with and tell them, in great detail, all your criteria. Let that person interface with the rest of the brokerage community on your behalf.

There are so many questions. Where do you want your building? How big? How many offices, how much warehouse space, etc.? Everything that is going to impact your business. Do you need special access to the highway or do you need foot or auto accommodations? These are just a few of the countless questions that will inevitably arise.

A good commercial real estate broker will first do a market survey and find what's out there. They'll check the listings. There's always a network of other brokers in the marketplace who know each other on a personal basis. Those brokers will be eager to share their listings with your broker.

There are also buyer brokers. This is a broker *you pay under a contract.* It's not a new concept—well, it might be in residential real estate, but it has gone on for decades commercially. The principal reason you would want one of these is because not everything that potentially can be purchased is necessarily going to be listed for sale. I have done many of these kinds of contracts, and clients have found it to be a very useful service.

It is very helpful to have a broker in your corner who has done twenty or thirty transactions this year and every year for the past twenty years. One who has been around the bend "a time or two" on purchase and sales contracts. A professional who is obligated to you and who has plenty of experience regarding what is reasonable. Such a buyer's broker can guide you as you negotiate, and, best of all, this dependable individual *works for you*.

Chapter Three

Making money is art and working is art and good business is the best art.

–Andy Warhol

Money Matters

F inancing is, of course, a major consideration in decisions about buying or constructing the building for your business. This is usually a substantial investment and expense, creating a lot of issues to consider. Key among them would be your source or sources of the financing you will need for this purchase. The terms will be very different, depending on which source you might use. Bank criteria will differ between types of bank, such as a local community bank—which might be more prone to serving as your lender—versus a regional or national commercial bank. The right choice can save you thousands of dollars.

This choice is not a simple matter of getting the interest rate at the best terms, although, of course, that's always part of your decision. There are more issues at stake that can help lead you to either success or failure.

Are the big national commercial banks the best way to go? Is bigger always better? Not necessarily. Having a solid relationship with your banker is far more important. It is crucial that you do your due diligence and find out how they have treated people in the past. Ask around, talk to other businesspeople, and find out what their banking experiences have been. Make no mistake about it, the big commercial banks do have a lot to offer, but they can also be very demanding and inflexible for a number of needs.

In many cases, smaller community banks with roots and their own future linked to the community might be not only friendlier, but more willing to work closely with you to address your particular concerns and find solutions when problems and obstacles arise. For some building purchases, when it comes to a lender, smaller is better. Again, this is just a matter of experience.

A variety of government programs are available that could make a difference in the property you purchase for your business. You may be eligible for a Small Business Administration (SBA) loan; the SBA even has a number of programs that can be applied to various business needs and purchases.

In essence, because an SBA loan is government-backed for a certain percentage, it offers you some advantages. Say you're a bit cash poor, needing your capital for inventory or development or any other important need. You might be able to get an SBA loan requiring only 10 percent down—in some cases, even less. Also, there's typically less paperwork and they will (believe it or not, this being a government agency) present fewer hoops for you to jump through in order to get the loan.

There are banks who are SBA-approved lenders, and they can do all the underwriting, so if they approve it, the SBA will also approve the loan. On the downside, the SBA does have its own criteria set by law that must be met, and there is not much wiggle room when it comes to exceptions.

In addition, every municipality and state has a variety of programs aimed at providing economic incentives to attract new or expanding businesses. Simply by crossing town or county lines, you could become eligible for a better deal or special incentive. Of course, you will only find out if a city, town, county is offering any such incentives to build in their town if you sit down with their planning people. Then there are areas designated as "enterprise zones." These areas hold specific incentives and may take several forms designed to entice you into purchasing and/or improving a building in that area, like a fixed period of reduced tax ownership.

Sometimes there are even outright grants available, which are essentially "free money" for which you may be eligible. Let's say a municipality is trying to build up their downtown area and they need a business such as yours. They may offer grants or other incentives in order to get the kind of businesses that they want in the neighborhood.

An often overlooked financing source is the seller of a property who fits the needs of your business. A seller often can offer a higher percentage loan to value than a lender can or more beneficial interest rate than you would get from a bank, even the one you already use for your business.

Here's an example: Say you locate a seller who might be willing to finance. You ask him (or her) what he is going to do with the money he gets from the sale. He may answer, "I am just going to put it in the bank."

A good strategy might be to make this kind offer: "Since you're only going to get less than 1 percent on your money in the bank, I will offer you four or five times that percentage if you provide me a mortgage on the building." This can strongly play to your advantage, especially since a bank is going to get you for the going rate plus points. If the owner accepts, you save some money and have an easier, smoother path to the closing.

Another option might be to buy another building of equal or greater value. The government says if you are just exchanging and you follow all the rules of section 1031 of the IRS tax code, the exchange becomes a tax-deferred event.

So, let's say I have a building worth $300,000. I tell my buyer I'm going to buy another building and I ask them to cooperate with me on a 1031 exchange.

This involves no financial concession at all on their part. In fact, it won't cost them anything, though there may be a few forms for them to sign.

Next, I go find a building for $750,000.

Finally, when I sell, my whole $300,000 of equity goes into the new building and any gain is tax-deferred. In this way, my equity gets to grow and appreciate without being diminished by paying taxes. Moreover, if I decide to sell it in the future, I can exchange it again and again, on and on, without paying tax.

In each case, the tax is deferred unless I stop and don't exchange. At that point, tax is paid on the capital gain as calculated on the final transaction.

If you're in a market with a trajectory that has been upward for several years and the economic outlook seems stable, you can count on the building steadily appreciating. Add that to your amortization and you will be in good shape.

Of course, things don't always go as projected or planned. Murphy's Law must always be taken into the equation. Managing risk is an important part of the process of buying that building, and one that many business owners fear. Yes, it can be a little nerve-wracking to contemplate investing in buying, designing, configuring, and owning a permanent home for your business. The added responsibilities—not just financial, but legal, maintenance, and related aspects that landlords handle—may seem daunting. This is another area where bringing in an expert can help resolve fears and provide answers to questions that will make the process go smoothly. Putting the process in the hands of experienced advisers will reduce risk on all levels and provide much-needed peace of mind as well.

The most common, and potentially most dangerous, aspect of buying a building for your business is going into the process without working with advisors who are experts in commercial real estate. Again, doing this oneself as the owner, or assigning the project—and it *is* a project—to a staffer, no matter how highly ranked in your business, is a huge risk.

Real-World Examples

The key to the successful purchase of a building for your business is a combination of expert advice and team building. Here are some examples of why it's smart to work with someone who understands commercial real estate and who can provide a long-term view that a business owner might not be able to see on their own.

Among the common pitfalls for an owner looking to purchase a building as a long-term home for the business is purchasing a building that doesn't meet the long-term needs of the business.

I had a client come to me after moving out of a rented building and into a building he bought and remodeled to fit his business. After only eighteen months in the new building, the business had already outgrown the owned space.

This is what I call a high-class problem: having to deal with selling the building and paying off the loan on it versus renting it out while you look for new, better space.

In another instance, a client was renting and wanted to buy a building. His business was in 2,500 square feet of space and he wanted us to build a new space of 6,000 square feet for him. I said he needed more space than that because it made sense to count on success—on his business continuing to thrive and grow—rather than to impose limitations on the future.

The client insisted on his original concept, so we built the new building for him as requested. A mere thirty days after he moved into the space he realized that the business had outgrown it!

Luckily for this client, we had another property nearby just like it that he could rent. For three years, the owner and some of his staff literally ran back and forth between the two properties on a daily basis to keep the business going until he could purchase a new building that was large enough to accommodate his current *and* future needs for space.

Had these clients consulted me (or taken my advice!) before buying their buildings, they might have purchased ones that offered space for growth. Generally, such issues can be mitigated with proper planning. If you have more space than you need at the moment, you can always use the excess for storage, or rent it out to someone else until you need it.

Here's an example of one organizational client who made good decisions about purchasing a building for their business. I was on the board of a charity that needed 16,000 square feet of space. I helped with securing tax free bond financing, found a lot, and suggested building a 22,000-square-foot building. The rationale was that the organization already had the bond funds in hand at a super-low interest rate, which meant that starting with a larger building would be a lot less expensive than having to go back and add space later.

We suggested building a shell for the whole space and only finishing the 16,000 square feet needed at the time. Less than a year later, the organization came back to us and said they needed the remaining space. Finishing it only cost $168,000—a *lot* less than if they had to build again to add more space. Had they not needed more room so soon, the organization could have rented out the unused area.

Another success story involves a group of engineers whose company owned a building they wanted to sell. It was part of a parcel of several properties that they owned—a parking lot, an old house across an alley, and the business site itself—that was worth about $750,000 as a whole. A neighbor was interested in buying the house for $84,000. I told them that the worst thing they could do was to sell that piece, because it represented space they could use as more parking. If they sold it, they would severely limit their ability to expand or restructure in the future, and they might face unpredictable problems with whoever purchased it.

A few years later, they were able to sell the whole property for $1 million because they tore down the house and added that space to their parking lot, which made the property more attractive to a buyer. Had they gone with Plan A, they might have had a small boost to the bank account at the time, but far less success in selling when they did. They profited substantially from a strategic plan with room for growth.

In general, the building you buy for your business will be a lot bigger than your house, so there are more aspects to the process—the size of the ground, the site itself, access to and egress from it, boundaries, environmental aspects, title matters, easements, and more. There are building codes to consider, traffic issues, community input and expectations, and so on—none of which arise when buying a house or even renting a business site. The building and its overall site will be your property, but the phone and electric company will have rights of access. All these various pieces must line up—again, the Rubik's Cube approach to commercial real estate. I used to rack my brains trying to figure out how to do a Rubik's Cube. Until I read a book on how to do it. As soon as I learned a couple of key secrets, it was a snap. And so, the analogy is drawn.

These examples demonstrate why it is important to work with someone who has been there and done that—someone who knows what to do, knows the real estate industry, has done corporate relocation, and has bought and sold (even built) properties. You need someone on your side—ideally, a team of experts—who is objective, experienced, knowledgeable, and future-oriented.

Chapter Four

Great things in business are never done by one person. They're done by a team of people.

–Steve Jobs

Building Your Team

Purchasing your building is clearly a complicated process, no matter how urgent and how potentially rewarding it might be. Your first step is to assemble a strong team to work on your behalf. These must be reliable professionals who can help you go about buying your building and avoiding the pitfalls that await you in this process. You *need* this dream team, more than you have probably realized. Here's a snapshot of the team you need on your side, with further detail below.

- An accountant
- A real estate attorney
- A commercial real estate broker
- A bank with a strong commercial real estate department
- A consultant

In forming this team, think about Newton's concept of light: a white light actually encompasses all the colors of the rainbow. When seen through a prism, the white light is broken down into individual colors. Likewise, you need individuals with different skills and experience to guide and help you through this process. Here are the members of the team you should assemble and the skills they should bring to the table.

Your **CPA**, but perhaps even better, a separate professional in accounting whose experience includes commercial real estate transactions, since these are quite different from the day-to-day business activities that your accountant or CFO usually handles. There's a big difference between handling day-to-day matters of employment, payroll, and taxes and purchasing a commercial building.

As we know, being an accountant or even a CPA in and of itself may not be enough to get you through this purchase or construction of a new business property. There's no one-size-fits-all in most professions today. Now more than ever, specialization is necessary and advisable.

For example, if your accountant is not steeped in real estate experience, he or she might fail to tell you about something like Section 1031 of the Internal Revenue code. Remember this? It's the matter of capital gains. If you are selling a property and then you are going to buy or build a new property of equal or greater value, you are able to defer the capital gains if you are going to use the money from the sale (including the profit) to buy/build the new building. To be clear, I am not in the business of giving tax advice, but I *am* in the business of advising you to get a good accountant who is thoroughly familiar and experienced with not just real estate, but commercial real estate.

When you consider the money involved in a commercial building, any mistake in buying the real estate can cost you not only money, but a *lot* of money, so it certainly behooves you to make sure that your team consists of people with the right knowledge and experience for their role in the transaction.

The **attorney** for your business, or again to be more specific, an attorney who practices in real estate, is essential, because there is also a difference between the legal aspects of a commercial property purchase and the routine legal activities of running your business. You want someone on your team—on your side—who understands the legal aspects of the real estate market and its complexities. Purchasing a building is, again, a far different process from renting one, with similarly different legal issues and concerns. You need someone who understands and who can protect you from the potential legal pitfalls that can make or break a deal, both while you're shopping and once you're in the building operating your business.

The basic lesson here is not to necessarily use the same attorney that you have used for your other business or personal affairs. Unless, of course, this person is thoroughly experienced in real estate. The law is so complicated and involved, you really need a seasoned pro with extensive real estate experience.

A **commercial real estate broker** is essential to this process as well. This professional will help you identify what kind of space your business needs and which properties are worth considering. This is someone who is familiar with what is on the market in your area and what you will need to do to make the right choice for your needs among the potential sites and properties available. You don't want to use a residential broker who is excited to work with you, because he or she usually sells houses for $200,000, and you're going to spend $2 million!

An experienced commercial real estate broker will not only know where to find appropriate properties for your business, but they can also recommend good lawyers, accountants, and other potential team members, including architects, engineers, and other professionals who will be important to your project once you have found the ideal property to buy. A broker at this level will be familiar with the local city planning board and can help you with any financial incentives or grants being offered, as well as dealing with the building inspector and other bureaucrats.

So, how do you identify such a real estate broker? First, if they are any good, they are going to have two or more certifications in the real estate industry—such as a CCIM, SIOR, or CRE, for a start. Then, they should be experienced. So, a second-year person should be considered a rookie (even with a certification or two) and would not be suitable. You need more experience. This individual must be someone who has been around the commercial market for many years. Whether you get the best or the worst agent, it's still going to cost you the same commission, so why not get the best?

The **right banker**. You need someone you can talk to (some are far more aloof than others!). Do you like the person; do they like you? Can you have a conversation? For example, if you ask if you can talk to someone off the record and their reply is "sure," this is a person you can work with, someone who is not going to tie you up with endless procedures and rules. You might be working with the local branch of a national company, which will mean decisions may take longer to get made. Patience (within reason) is called for sometimes. It's also a good idea if he or she belongs to as many professional organizations as possible.

An **independent consultant** can bring all these elements into play, unified on your behalf for the benefit of your business. Someone in this role will vet the other professionals you need on your team, focus on the potential future of your business, develop a plan for or approach to finding the kind of property you need, and perhaps discard suggestions from other team members that don't fit your goals and needs. As an independent, this person works for you and your business—not for the bank, the mortgage broker, or the owner of a property you might want to select.

A consultant's role can depend on the services you need—you may need someone who functions as your team leader, but you also may need an environmental or architectural consultant at various points in the process. One very important consultant is your insurance agent. You need someone who is more than just an agent, someone who has lots of experience in insuring commercial buildings and who knows all the liabilities that can befall you, some you have never heard of or probably would never even consider. Don't forget, the owner of a commercial building will be viewed as having "deep pockets" and will be prey to anybody who breaks a fingernail in or near your building. You shouldn't have just enough insurance to satisfy your lender but enough to protect you and your future.

The consultant does these things instead of the broker if the broker doesn't have the proper skill set and has not been trained in counseling. If the broker has been trained in counseling and understands the issues from a global perspective, then they can have this dual role.

Beyond an agent, you may want to consult with a public adjuster. That's because an insurance adjuster represents the insurance company—but who represents you? A public adjuster can do battle with a company adjuster and save you substantial amounts of money. Business owners often don't realize that public adjusters even exist, much less that they can help in purchasing the building your business needs.

You will also want to consult your peers, so your membership in a *professional association* could be the key to two vital aspects of this process—finding the team members you need and spreading the word about the kind of property you seek. Several will let you—or your consultant—vet members based on experience, track record, education, and more. Organizations worth considering include the Counselors of Real Estate (CRE), Society of Industrial and Office Real Estate (SIOR), Certified Commercial Investment Member of the National Association of REALTORS® (CCIM), the Society of Exchange Counselors (SEC), and the National Council of Real Estate Exchangers (NCE).

These organizations are a kind of club or insiders' group, where experienced members of the profession gather, learn from, and network with each other, sharing resources and insights. You might find out about a commercial property before it comes up on the open market, or benefit from an association discount on services or even the purchasing price.

Belonging to a professional association—or working with a consultant who belongs to one—can help ensure that your team members have the experience, track record, credentials, and references that you should require.

Be aware, however, that networking is a two-way street that works best if you invest time and effort into your membership and give as much as you take. Colleagues will be leery of anyone who joins a local real estate association one day and expects favored status the next day, before making any contributions to the organization in the way of participation in programs, committee or board service, and other aspects of going beyond "checkbook" membership.

Chapter Five

Begin with the end in mind.

–Stephen Covey

Resolving the Problems—How to Shop and Buy

Steps to take before making the actual purchase of a building start with an accurate assessment of what your needs really are; this is another area where your team will come into play and one that can be essential to your success.

Start by assessing how you are using your existing space, and then determine what you need to meet your current demands as well as for expansion and other uses in the future. This is where the process can get tricky, so give serious thought to this aspect. As we have discussed, think to the future.

Business owners often don't adequately project what their needs will be and don't always understand the challenge of designing space to fit both current and future needs. You can move a wall much more easily with a pen and paper (or computer design program) than after you buy or build the place and find that the layout doesn't actually work for your business.

For example, let's go back to a case I mentioned earlier. The daughters of a wealthy farmer wanted to be caterers, so they started a business while in college. Their father gave them a metal barn on the family farm to use as their business location, which they used until they decided to build their own place further out in the country. Using a residential realtor, they bought a farmhouse in a beautifully pastoral setting with several acres, planning to live in the house and run the business from a building with cutting-edge architecture and design. However, neither they nor their realtor knew that the property was not zoned for commercial use.

It was a real mess to unscramble that egg. They had to circulate petitions among nearby residents, appear before the county board, and get support from a super-majority before they could proceed with their business. It worked out eventually, but was a terrible risk, took up valuable time that could have been used to build and profit from the business, cost a lot of money in legal and other fees, and could easily have been ruinous. And all of the headaches, additional expenses, delays, and related hassles could have been avoided if they had done their due diligence, or at least worked with an appropriate service provider who would have checked on details like zoning and permitted use before actually making the purchase of the property.

Before making any purchase decisions, an experienced advisor would check with local zoning and planning offices—they are usually delighted to support business projects, so long as you follow the rules. And you can't follow rules that you haven't looked into.

Due diligence is a specific term that relates to being able to close a transaction. It is used to express a process and period of time for a buyer to confirm all of the facts relevant to that purchase. During that period is when you (or your representatives) look into regulations, permitting, zoning, and related rules, as well as when you would perform property inspections—mechanical, roof, plumbing, heating/cooling systems, etc.

There are no rules or regulations for whom to use for these inspections, but a skilled consultant will be able to provide input on what to look for in those professionals. Don't use "good ol' Uncle Joe"! I strongly recommend using a professional inspector who, like your commercial real estate broker, is experienced in the business sector. In most, if not all, states, professional inspectors have to be licensed. There are many franchises in this sector, most of which provide training for their franchisees.

You also might have to hire an engineering firm. Again, you don't want to use a residential firm, although some will do light commercial work such as for a small office property.

To ensure the roof of the building you plan to purchase is safe, secure, and stable, for instance, you can work with independent tradespeople such as a local roofing company. For electrical systems and HVAC, you need to be sure that that proper calculations have been made for the number of BTUs the business will need, as well as a safe system of air exchange. Foundation and structural matters are quite complex and also require input from experts.

A large part of due diligence is an official boundary survey. If there's a fence on the property, it might actually be on a neighboring property. There could be issues of rights to full use of not only your potential building but also the land on which it sits. There could be concerns about access as well.

This is more of a residential story than a business one, but it is relevant to this part of the process. A colleague bought a new house when he got married. A neighbor had a garden on the colleague's property and sued for adverse possession because she had used the land "openly and notoriously" for twenty years, even though it was on his land. He had to pay her $5,000 to move her garden so he could put up a fence around his property. Something similar could happen with a commercial property that you would like to own for your business.

Your attorney should check the title to the building you want to buy after your commercial real estate broker has found the ideal property for your business. The title work should include checking for defects, liens, disputes that have been recorded, taxes, etc. This might be an extreme example, but, for instance, the U.S. Drug Enforcement Administration (DEA) could have a lien against the building because the seller was a drug dealer—although the issues are more commonly unpaid loan balances, mechanics' liens, or unpaid back taxes.

Once a clear title has been established, stop and think about how you want to hold title to the property. Consider owning the building under your name rather than in the name of the business, and leasing it back to the business. That could be beneficial from a tax perspective, as well as in the ability to sell the building but keep the property in the future.

Say you lease the building back to the company. It's kind of a forced retirement payment because every lease payment pays down the mortgage. And it might be easier when you sell your company later if you still own the building and can lease it out.

It can take time to perform due diligence and check out the many aspects of a building purchase, so be wary of a seller who seems to be in too much of a hurry to complete the transaction. Yes, you want to make the purchase and move forward with tailoring and occupying the new home for your business, but you don't want to be pressured into skipping any of the steps that could result in disaster after the papers have been signed.

Here's a practical suggestion for risk management: When you are ready to make the purchase, you need proper contingencies in place so you are not under any final obligation to pay until all such contingencies have been met. That should include confirmation that the building and property are zoned for your use and there will be no objections to your business making its home there. This is, again, where a good attorney and broker will know how to structure the deal on your behalf.

Surveys

A land survey is made for the title company and/or the lender with the survey and location data needed for the issuance of title or mortgage insurance. For this purpose, a map is drawn to American Land Title Association (ALTA) specifications.

ALTA specifies the date to be shown on the survey and the boundary lines, location of the main building including improvements, location of ancillary buildings, and the identification of easements (access rights by service companies such as water, gas, telephone, railways, and other utilities). ALTA surveys are quite comprehensive, can cost tens of thousands of dollars, and take weeks to complete. For that reason, ALTA surveys are most often reserved for commercial properties.

Besides meeting the ALTA requirements, an ALTA land survey guarantees that you meet the requirements of the National Society of Professional Surveys and the American Congress on Surveying and Mapping.

Of course, this is pretty much reserved for fairly expensive properties. And what is "expensive" is of course a subjective, commonsense kind of decision for the purchaser to determine.

Such surveys are worth the cost, however, because of how thoroughly exacting they are, encompassing any easements, encroachments, and title defects as well as an inspection of all mechanical aspects of the building including plumbing, electric, HVAC, etc.

Often, as a condition of purchase, you can ask the seller to foot the bill for this survey.

Another good reason for doing this type of in-depth survey is that, when you go to sell the building some years down the road, you will know of any potential complications. For example, somebody could have access rights to the property. There can in many cases be old deeds that have some bearing as to what you can do on the property. For instance, let's say that at some time after purchase, you decide you need to build a garage on the property. You may find that the location where you want to build the garage is over sewer lines that the city needs access to in case they have to dig them up. That could pose a major headache that could have been avoided by being cautious enough to have taken this one extra step.

Talking to other building owners in the neighborhood is always a good idea, too. You may learn things that you otherwise might not have. Perhaps a train goes through the area much more frequently (and disruptively!) than you had realized. Again, it would be highly preferable to know this important information prior to making the decision to buy.

It is possible that only a boundary survey is sufficient. But make sure about that. The best way to protect yourself is to structure the deal properly in the first place.

Environmental Risk

Assessing environmental risk is an important aspect of any real estate acquisition. It is not my intent in this guide to give legal advice. Let me just say that putting yourself into the chain of title on tainted real estate can significantly increase your liability. It is here that a good environmental engineer can be a vital member of your team.

The good news is that there is no need to put yourself in jeopardy. There are many steps you can take to mitigate risk where environmental matters are concerned.

This guide, while not comprehensive, seeks to raise your awareness of the issue and its impact on your decision-making process. And offer a few suggestions as to what you can do to protect yourself from exposure.

Here are some of the reports that are common in the industry that you should familiarize yourself with:

Desktop Reports

An Environmental Desktop Report is a limited-scope assessment that does not include a visit by the environmental consultant to the subject property – hence the term "desktop." the desktop report is often used as a cost-effective initial screen of a property to determine the potential for environmental liability at the site, such as contamination from a nearby gas station. If such a concern is identified, then often the evaluation is elevated to a more comprehensive report such as the Phase I ESA report.

The environmental risk of the subject site is evaluated through a review of records and pertinent information that may include:

- Government records (a database search and/or other regulatory records)
- Historical records such as Sanborn fire insurance maps, city directories, aerial photos, and topographic maps
- Environmental questionnaires

Phase I Environmental Site Assessment

A Phase I ESA should be conducted in general accordance with ASTM Standard E-1527-13 at the project site and assess commonly known and reasonably ascertainable information. The scope of the Phase I ESA will include the following tasks:

- Conduct a record review utilizing EDR Radius Map Report (an EDR Radius Map Report is a report which documents a database search of available public databases for historic environmental incidents within a designated radius of your site)

- Review reasonably ascertainable standard sources for generalized geology as deemed appropriate by the Environmental Professional

- Review topographic maps utilizing EDR Historical Topographic Map Report

- Review reasonably ascertainable standard sources for groundwater data as deemed appropriate by the Environmental Professional

- Review reasonably ascertainable standard sources for soil information as deemed appropriate by the Environmental Professional

- Review coal mining directory information

- Review historical seismic activity information

- Review aerial photographs utilizing EDR Aerial Photograph Report

- Review available Sanborn Fire Insurance Maps utilizing EDR Sanborn Report

- Review available City Directory utilizing EDR City Directory Report

- Conduct a Site Reconnaissance visit inclusive of photographic documentation and observation write-up

- Conduct interview with a Key Site manager for the Subject Property which may be Owner, Occupants, etc.

as deemed appropriate by the Environmental Professional

- Conduct interview with local official regarding the subject property as deemed appropriate by the Environmental Professional

- Prepare a report detailing the findings and conclusions of the Environmental Site Assessment

Limited Soil and Water Investigations

Phase II ESA report

After the completion of a Phase I ESA there sometimes are historical discoveries that suggest further investigation would be recommended to understand the potential for the presence or absence of contaminates of concern. Phase I ESA's do not involve sampling, so the next step of environmental investigation often involves the sampling of soil and groundwater.

The initial sampling is typically limited to an immediate area of concern. The samples are then sent to a laboratory to be tested for the contaminates that may be present on a property because of past land use.

Although there is a process for a full Phase II sampling investigation, additional sampling beyond the initial sampling is typically reserved for conditions related to meeting environmental compliance investigations. In the event that limited sampling and review of site conditions indicates that there is a "Recognized Environmental Condition" (REC) present at the site, a full Phase II ESA may be undertaken, with the focus being to determine the condition of the site relative to environmental compliance under the regulatory framework of the site, typically the State Environmental Protection Agency.

Just knowing the questions to ask about the environmental aspects of the real estate in question will put you way ahead of potential liability. Be sure that you ask those questions well in advance of a purchase. Your attorney (if he has environmental experience) can be a valuable asset to your team here. If your attorney does not have environmental experience, then a good environmental engineer can be invaluable. Just be sure you have a qualified team member on point with this issue.

After the purchase

Most of the hard work of buying a building for your business is done before and during due diligence. The right choice of attorney and real estate broker can be vital to ensuring that you have done the right amount of work in laying the groundwork for this process.

There is still more to do after the purchase has gone through, though.

Even from the day you move the business into the new building, you need to make sure to maintain both the building and the property well. Think in terms of what you need from the property now and in the future to ensure it will be more valuable when you are ready to sell years down the road.

The main thing to keep in mind for "after" the purchase is not to mess it up by adding new space or buildings without the proper due diligence, storing dangerous chemicals in the new place, or being a bad neighbor or community member in some way.

If you've done everything right, you should be able to have "quiet enjoyment" of the new property. All that is left to do is send out announcements about the new location of your business and hold a grand opening celebration!

One last useful thing is to maintain and store good records for the property. For example, you should keep a copy of the survey, deeds, floor plan, fire marshal evacuation report, and everything you have relative to that building, including manuals for the furnaces and HVAC systems and lighting plans. Keep a list of the original builder, the architects, etc. Create a digital file to go along with the hard copies. Ten years from now, what would have been difficult to assemble will be there at your fingertips, ready to facilitate an expansion or sale.

Resources

There are many resources for a business owner planning to purchase a building. I've listed just some of them below. Also, please see the appendix for a Due Diligence Checklist that I think you will find helpful.

CCIM Institute http://www.ccim.com/

American Land Title Association (ALTA)
https://www.alta.org/

National Association of REALTORS®
https://www.nar.realtor/

American Institute of Architects https://www.aia.org/

Appraisal Institute https://www.appraisalinstitute.org/

National Association of Industrial and Office Properties
http://www.naiop.org/

Building Owners and Managers Association (BOMA) International http://www.boma.org/

International Council of Shopping Centers (ICSC)
http://www.icsc.org/

Institute of Real Estate Management (IREM)
http://www.irem.org/

National Multi Housing Council (NMHC)
http://www.nmhc.org/

National Real Estate Investor http://nreionline.com/

Commercial Investment Real Estate Magazine
http://ciremagazine.com/

Counselors of Real Estate https://www.cre.org/

Society of Industrial and Office Realtors
http://www.sior.com/

The quotations provided on the first page of each chapter were found on www.BrainyQuotes.com.

About the Authors

Alex Ruggieri serves as a senior advisor for SVN, specializing in the sale of investment properties in Champaign-Urbana and Central Illinois. With over 40 years of commercial real estate industry experience. Ruggieri has secured a career sales volume of over $500 million. Ruggieri is a partner in Ramshaw Real Estate, a full-service brokerage firm, where he remains involved in acquisitions, sales, development, and management of various types of investment properties. Career highlights include being the recipient of the SVN Achievers Award for outstanding sales and the coveted Partner's Circle Award multiple years (the company's highest sales award!). Ruggieri is a Certified Commercial Investment Member (CCIM) of NAR and holds the prestigious Counselor of Real Estate (CRE) designation as well as the Certified International Property (CIPS) Specialist.

Noah Ruggieri has an MBA with a minor in corporate governance and international business from the University of Illinois. Attending Commercial Real Estate marketing conferences across the United States every eight weeks for many years has given him a unique perspective on the market, as well as connections with national Investors from all four corners of the county. Before entering real estate, he was self-employed for nine years and also worked in the financial sector for a national institution. A background in banking has only enhanced his knowledge base for helping clients as a commercial real estate counselor. Noah has given back to the community over the years through volunteer work with a local BSA scouting group as well as mentoring in the CU 1to1 Program for multiple years. An avid family man he cherishes free time with his wife and two daughters.

Appendix

Acquisition of Real Estate - Comprehensive Due Diligence Checklist

The acquisition of real estate involves a myriad of issues which should be addressed by the purchaser and its counsel. The following outline is created to serve as a due diligence checklist for such acquisition. The checklist is not intended to, and cannot, include state and local regulations or practices, but rather is an attempt to raise the practitioner's level of consciousness on issues of general application. The reader should investigate state and local requirements as well.

I. GENERAL INFORMATION

A. Determine address and location of the property; obtain any applicable tax identification numbers, subdivision parcel numbers and other governmental designations of the property.

B. Identify record owner of the property and period of ownership. Obtain information on Seller's domicile or company or company directors - Citizen of? Obtain Seller's I.D. number or Company registration number.

C. Determine past record owners of the property for at least 60 years (obtain name and period of ownership for each).

D. Identify present tenants and subtenants of the property.

E. Determine past tenants and subtenants of the property (obtain name and period of tenancy for each).

F. Identify all present uses of the property.

G. Obtain description of the property, as follows:

    1. Size of the property (acres or square meters).

    2. Number of buildings at the property.

    3. For each building provide:

        a. number of stories and square meter per story

        b. kind of construction (e.g., brick, wood, steel, etc.)

        c. age

        d. current use and prior uses (indicate time period for each prior use)

4. For any previous building on the property obtain:

    a. date demolished

    b. uses (indicate time period for each use)

5. Determine and describe any structures currently on the property other than buildings (such as water towers, above ground tanks, cellular phone towers, high tension wire towers, etc.).

6. Determine and describe any structures other than buildings previously on the property (include relevant time periods).

H. Identify (if any) person responsible for environmental matters at the property.

II. TITLE AND SURVEY

A. Obtain from seller and evaluate copies of all title insurance policies, title insurance reports, attorneys' title certifications; if available from Seller all documents and/or title exceptions referred to therein.

B. Obtain from seller copy of deed by which seller acquired its interest in the property, if in fee simple, or deed or assignment by which seller acquired leasehold interest, if subject to ground lease. Obtain from seller other documents relating to its acquisition of the property - acquisition agreements, settlement sheets, due diligence items.

C. Order new title search and obtain title insurance commitment insuring purchaser (including appropriate affirmative coverage endorsements). Obtain from title agent copies of all documents and exceptions described in title insurance commitment. Order judgment searches and lien sheets. Evaluate condition of title, all title exceptions, and reports of all such searches, and determine if any lis pendens exist. Consider whether to competitively bid title insurance where premiums and fees not covered by state filings. Consider need for reinsurance and direct access agreements for the benefit of purchaser. Determine what title policy endorsements are available, and at what cost.

D. Obtain from seller copies of all existing surveys and plats, surveyor's reports and surveyor's certifications.

E. Order new surveys or updates of existing surveys for the property, as appropriate; among other things, current boundaries, all existing and proposed improvements, all parking spaces, all present and proposed utility lines and systems, and all easements, rights-of-way, restrictions, encroachments, setback lines, and other title exceptions. Surveys should be accompanied by certifications as to survey matters in a form acceptable to purchaser. Evaluate surveys and all conditions shown on surveys. Have surveyor prepare a metes and bounds description of the property.

F. Obtain estoppel certificate from the ground lessor, if applicable, confirming terms of ground lease and non-existence of defaults or specifying defaults. Determine if Ground Lessor consent is required. Obtain such consent if required. Consider need to amend ground lease, and if necessary, amend ground lease to purchaser's satisfaction at or prior to settlement. Consider need to obtain non-disturbance protection from any fee mortgagee.

G. Confirm direct access, for purposes of vehicular and pedestrian ingress and egress, of the property to a public street or roadway. If no direct access, evaluate alternatives, including availability of easements.

H. Obtain from seller evidence of compliance of the property with all applicable private restrictions and covenants (recorded and unrecorded), and procure any required approvals prior to settlement.

I. Confirm at or prior to settlement that all mortgages, deeds of trust and other liens encumbering the property (other than those mortgages and/or deeds of trust, if any, to be assumed at settlement by purchaser or as to which title will be taken subject to) have been satisfied and released of record or arrangements for releases have been made.

III. REAL PROPERTY TAXES AND OTHER GOVERNMENTAL IMPOSITIONS

A. Obtain from seller and evaluate:

1. Copies of current bills showing all real property taxes, agricultural taxes, other ordinary and special assessments, water and sewer charges and other impositions.

2. Copies of all current notices of real property tax assessments and assessments as to any special or other impositions.

3. Copies of any notices or letters advising of pending reassessments or forthcoming special assessments.

4. Copies of any pleadings, filings, notices and/or other correspondence pertaining to challenges, appeals or

other proceedings concerning real property tax matters, special assessments and other governmental impositions.

5. Copies of any agreements with governmental or taxing authorities concerning the deferral or reduction of real property taxes or other impositions, or payments in lieu of taxes.

6. Information concerning any special taxing districts in which the property is located.

B. Conduct independent investigation to confirm all applicable governmental impositions for real property taxes, special assessments, water, sewer, and other charges, and to determine likelihood of any pending or future reassessments or special assessments. Consider feasibility of entering into tax incentive agreements (such as payments in lieu of taxes) with local governments. Determine whether the property is subject to agricultural assessment.

C. Investigate whether any statutory abatement of taxes affects the property.

IV. ZONING, SUBDIVISION AND LAND USE MATTERS

A. Obtain from seller and evaluate:

1. Evidence of current zoning and land use classifications and compliance of the property with respect to zoning, subdivision and land use laws and regulations;

2. Copies of all applicable subdivision approvals, special exceptions, variances, and other governmental legislative and administrative actions concerning zoning, land use and subdivision matters;

3. Copies of all violation notices, notices of pending rezoning or land use reclassifications, and all pleadings or filings pertaining to zoning, subdivision or land use actions or proceedings;

4. Copies of any opinions of counsel as to zoning, subdivision or land use matters in the possession of seller;

5. Copies of any agreements, orders or decrees concerning impact fees, linkage fees, exactions, adequate public facilities charges or similar fees or charges;

6. Copies of any agreements relating to growth management or adequate public facilities laws or regulations; and

7. Copies of any agreements or proposed deeds with respect to any contemplated dedication or proffers to any governmental agency or private body of any portions of any of the properties;

B. Conduct independent investigation to determine compliance of the property with applicable zoning, subdivision and land use laws and regulations.

1. Review all applicable laws, rules, regulations, agreements, orders and approvals.

2. Consider need for opinions of counsel.

3. Consider need for title insurance zoning endorsements.

4. Obtain comfort as to absence of pending zoning or land use reclassifications and any other legislative or

administrative actions which might adversely affect the property, its zoning, subdivision or land use status, or purchaser's contemplated uses.

5. Confirm with surveyor compliance of the property with respect to any applicable setback requirements.

6. Consider applicability of any state or local adequate public facilities, smart growth, or other growth management legislation, moratoria, and impact fees, linkage charges or exactions, whether currently enacted or contemplated, particularly as to any contemplated construction on or improvement of the property.

7. Determine any contemplated dedication or proffers of any portions of the property to any governmental agency or private body.

C. Consider meeting with local community or citizens groups and local zoning officials to explain the conveyance of the property from seller to purchaser and any particular plans that purchaser may have after conveyance, such as expansion or new construction.

V. STRUCTURAL SUFFICIENCY AND CONSTRUCTION

A. Obtain from seller copies of as-built plans and specifications for the property.

B. Obtain copies of all warranties still in effect; determine assignability.

C. Obtain and evaluate a comprehensive study of the physical condition of the property, prepared by an engineer or consultant selected by purchaser. Procure from seller copies of any such studies previously obtained by seller. Consider need for any repairs or replacements, as revealed by such studies, and reach agreement with seller as to allocation of costs thereof.

D.   Obtain from seller copies of any building code violation notices or other violation notices pertaining to the property. If any such violations exist, reach agreement with seller as to responsibility for amelioration prior to settlement and as to payment of costs of amelioration.

E.   If there is any present or contemplated construction or improvement of the property, obtain from seller:

1. copies of plans and specifications;

2. copies of all construction contracts, major subcontracts, and architectural services agreements;

3. copies of approvals from all required governmental agencies and private entities (e.g., building permits, environmental approvals, approvals of ground lessors);

4. copies of any payment and performance bonds;

5. copies of construction budget and project cost breakdowns; and

6. copies of engineering feasibility studies, soil tests, and borings.

7. Determine whether purchaser should require that construction be completed prior to settlement, and if not, identify the conditions pertaining to uncompleted construction to be met as of settlement.

F. Obtain from seller copies of pleadings, settlement agreements and relevant correspondence pertaining to any pending or threatened litigation relating to ongoing or completed construction at the property.

G. Confirm at or immediately prior to settlement that no mechanics' liens or materialmen's liens have been filed with respect to the property. Obtain from seller at or before settlement all affidavits, indemnities, and waivers of liens of contractors in this regard that purchaser or title insurer shall require.

H. Conduct independent investigation to determine whether any existing building code violations or other violations exist with respect to the property. Resolve with seller responsibility for making of all ameliorations prior to settlement and for the payment for all costs of amelioration.

I. If property is residential property, investigate presence of lead paint; determine cost of removal.

J. Consider conducting a termite inspection (may be required by lender for residential property); consider conducting a radon inspection.

K. Determine whether smoke detector, sprinkler or similar ordinances are applicable to the property.

VI. TENANTS AND SUBTENANTS

A. Obtain complete copies of all leases, including all amendments, addenda, exhibits, side agreements, lease abstracts, etc. Inquire as to credit worthiness of each tenant

B. Obtain copies of all lease commission agreements.

C. Obtain copies of the most up-to-date rent roll including the following by tenant:

   1. Tenant name and suite number;

   2. Square footage (both rentable and usable);

   3. Lease commencement date;

   4. Lease expiration date;

   5. Listing of options;

   6. Annual and monthly base rent including steps;

   7. Responsibility for taxes, insurance, operating expense stops, base year information;

   8. Security deposits;

   9. Rent concessions;

  10. Rights of first offer or refusal;

  11. Expansion options;

  12. Cancellation clauses;

  13. Any other preferential clauses or restrictions (e.g., signage, exclusive, etc.);

  14. Responsibility for maintenance, repairs, casualty losses;

  15. Obligations of parties to make improvements permitted use.

D. Obtain copies of all real estate tax bills, reassessments and correspondence for the preceding five years.

E. Obtain copies of all personal property tax bills and correspondence for the preceding five years.

F.   Obtain copies of all utility bills for current and prior two years, and relevant correspondence (e.g. utility energy savings programs). Obtain a list of the location and purpose of each meter.

G.   Obtain detailed map of property, including at least the following:

   1. Site plan;

   2. Floor-by-floor space plan locating each tenant and vacant space;

   3. Individual space plans identifying constructed improvements;

   4. As-built plans.

H.   Obtain copies of tenant escalation (real estate taxes, and insurance) billing worksheets that show the calculations including base year information, stops, etc.

I.   Obtain copies of all service contracts including a brief description of its purpose and current amount being paid.

J.   Obtain itemized list of operating expenses for the prior five years.

K.   Obtain year-to-date financial statements including the current year's operating and capital budgets.

L.   Obtain year-end financial statements and audit reports for the prior two years.

M.   Obtain current schedule of any tenant improvement work not started.

N.   Obtain current on-going construction contracts.

O. Obtain copies of notices regarding violation of ordinances.

P. Obtain description and cost of major additions, deletions and renovations completed or anticipated.

Q. Obtain any required compliance survey, engineering reports and environmental reports, if available.

R. Obtain copies of latest building inspection reports and certificates of occupancy for the building shell and for each tenant space.

S. Obtain any information relating to the soil condition in respect to the property.

T. Obtain copies of park covenants and approvals for the building if located in an office or industrial park.

U. Obtain from each tenant and subtenant an estoppel certificate:

   1. Confirming lease or sublease and important details of the tenancy; and

   2. Confirming non-existence of defaults or specifying defaults; and

   3. Confirming the non-existence of any bankruptcy or similar proceedings by or against the tenant.

V. Determine whether there are any statutory rights of first refusal in favor of any tenants.

VII. UTILITIES

A. Obtain from seller and evaluate evidence of sources and availability of all required utilities (e.g., electricity, gas, water, sewer, steam, telephone).

B.   Obtain from seller and evaluate copies of any applicable governmental or private agreements concerning availability of, or hook-up to, required utilities.

C.   Conduct independent investigation to confirm availability and sufficiency of all required utilities.

VIII. INSURANCE

A.   Obtain evidence from seller that the property is adequately covered by insurance satisfactory to purchaser. Seek increases in coverages if inadequate.

B.   Obtain evidence that purchaser has been added as an additional insured during the contract period, to the extent of its interests, with respect to each policy of insurance maintained by seller for the property.

C.   Determine whether the property is located in an area designated as having special flood risks and, if so designated, obtain available flood insurance.

D.   Obtain from seller reports as to any existing or threatened litigation concerning insurance claims with respect to the property, together with copies of all pleadings, settlement agreements and other relevant documentation.

E.   Obtain comfort at settlement that the property has not suffered a casualty loss prior to settlement which has not been properly and fully repaired at seller's expense. If repairs are incomplete, confirm arrangements for completion of work, at seller's expense (or alternatively, at purchaser's expense with a sufficient credit at settlement).

F.   Obtain insurance coverage at or prior to settlement protecting purchaser with respect to:

1. fire and other casualties and hazards on the buildings, improvements and contents;

2. flood insurance (if applicable);

3. public liability insurance;

4. plate glass insurance (if desired);

5. business interruption insurance (if desired);

6. rent insurance (if desired); and

7. any other insurance desired by purchaser.

G.   Evaluate applicable deductibles and self-insurance.

IX. FINANCING TO BE ASSUMED BY PURCHASER (IF ANY).

A.   Obtain copies of all notes, mortgages, deeds of trust, security agreements and other loan documents with respect to any existing financing to be assumed (including taking title subject to existing financing) by purchaser as part of acquisition.

B.   Review and evaluate all such loan and mortgage documentation to determine:

1. feasibility of assumption by purchaser; (e.g., due on sale or encumbrance) and consent by mortgagee;

2. conditions pertaining to assumption by purchaser;

3. any applicable fees or penalties; and

4. any modifications desired by purchaser as a condition of assumption.

C. Obtain estoppel certificate from each such mortgagee or lender:

    1. confirming important details of each such financing;

    2. confirming outstanding principal balance; and

    3. confirming non-existence of defaults or specifying defaults.

        a. Obtain any required modifications in anticipation of settlement.

X. CONDEMNATION

A. Obtain from seller and evaluate copies of any notices or correspondence regarding pending or threatened condemnation of the property.

B. Conduct independent investigation to determine whether any condemnations are pending or threatened with respect to the property. If any such actions are pending or imminent, consider effect on transaction.

XI. APPRAISALS

    A. Obtain from seller copies of all existing appraisals for the property. If desired or necessary, obtain and evaluate new appraisals for the property satisfactory in form to purchaser and any lender.

XII. PERMITS AND LICENSES

A. Obtain from seller copies of all permits, licenses and governmental approvals (other than environmental permits) maintained by seller in connection with its operation of the property.

B. Conduct independent investigation to determine nature of all permits, licenses and approvals required in connection with the contemplated operation of the property by purchaser.

C. Consider feasibility of transfer and/or assignment of any existing permits, licenses and approvals from seller to purchaser. Obtain new permits, licenses, no violation letters and approvals as required.

XIII. PROPERTY AGREEMENTS

A. Obtain from seller copies of all agreements pertaining to seller's use or operation of the property, including management agreements, contracts providing for removal of snow and ice and/or refuse, agreements pertaining to the maintenance of the property, contracts relating to the maintenance and/or replacement of systems serving the property, and public works agreements and any unrecorded agreements with any governmental agency.

B. Determine feasibility of assigning any contracts described in the preceding subparagraph from seller to purchaser at settlement, if so desired by purchaser. Consider rights of termination and any applicable fees or charges for termination.

C. Obtain comfort that purchaser will, at settlement or within a reasonable time thereafter, be able to enter into all property agreements deemed by seller to be necessary in connection with its use and/or operation of the property.

D. Evaluate feasibility of assignment at settlement by seller to purchaser of any warranties with respect to the roof and equipment at the property.

E. Obtain from seller copies of all listing agreements for rentals at the property; determine whether commissions will be due from purchaser in the event of renewal of any lease.

XIV. COMPLIANCE INVESTIGATION

A. Conduct an audit of the property's systems technology to determine whether the technology is able to accurately process date/time data (including, but not limited to, calculating, comparing and sequencing).

XV. PERSONAL PROPERTY

A. Obtain from seller a listing of any personal property utilized by seller in connection with its operation of the property which will be conveyed to purchaser.

B. Obtain from seller copies of all bills of sale and other documentation pursuant to which title to any personal property to be conveyed to purchaser became vested in seller.

C. At or prior to settlement obtain from seller evidence that title to any such personal property will be assigned to purchaser at settlement free and clear of all liens and security interests.

XVI. HISTORIC PROPERTY DESIGNATIONS

A. Obtain from seller copies of all orders, decrees, special legislative enactments or agreements enacted by or made with or by any federal, state or local government or agency concerning the designation of the property as historic, as a landmark, or as being subject to any similar classification.

B. Conduct independent investigation to determine whether any of the properties have been designated, or are likely in the future to be designated, as historic properties, as landmarks, or as being subject to any similar classification. Consider the impact of such designations or potential designations upon the value of the property being acquired and any contemplated plans for construction or improvements of those properties.

XVII. ADJUSTMENTS

A. Consider the financial adjustments which will have to be made at settlement in connection with acquisition of the property, including without limitation, adjustments as to real property taxes and other governmental impositions, utility charges and service contracts.

B. Consider the cost of any taxes and other charges payable in connection with the conveyance of the property, and the recordation of the deed or other documents at settlement.

XVIII. ENVIRONMENTAL MATTERS - OBTAIN WITH RESPECT TO THE PROPERTY INFORMATION AND DOCUMENTS, AND CONDUCT AN INDEPENDENT INVESTIGATION, TO ADDRESS ISSUES SPECIFIED BELOW

A. Physical Condition of Property

   1. Underground Storage Tanks

a. Any currently existing aboveground or underground storage tanks, or tanks previously located at the property, providing the following for each:

- size

- construction;

- age (or age at removal or closure);

- current and past uses, including the time period for each use;

- if no longer in use, determine abandonment/closure/removal procedure

- compliance with applicable registration and tank maintenance, testing and safety requirements.

2. Determine and describe any lakes, lagoons, impoundments, pits, septic tanks, trenches, dry wells, catch basins, ditches, trenches, or other open conduits that are or have been on the property, providing for each:

a. size;

b. nature of material contained in or conveyed;

c. liners and detection systems; and

d. description of any dams, dikes or embankments.

3. Determine and describe any pipelines now or previously on the property, including size and materials transported, when constructed, and type.

4. Determine and describe any locations on the property where any materials, wastes, or substances have been released or disposed of, providing for each:

   a. size;

   b. when disposal or release occurred;

   c. nature of material waste or substance; and

   d. nature of disposal or release.

   e. any remedial action that took place

5. Determine any unusual land or soil coloration or other unusual conditions at the property and obtain an explanation.

6. Determine any stressed or unusual vegetation or physical irregularities that might indicate unusual subsurface conditions or disposal of wastes, and obtain an explanation.

7. Determine any areas on the property which would be or have been designated under federal, state or local regulations as wetlands, flood plains, coastal areas, habitat for endangered species or historical/archeological sites (location, size, type).

B. Ongoing Operations at Property

   1. Determine and describe any hazardous materials and/or hazardous waste management facilities at the property, including treatment, storage, disposal and recycling facilities.

   2. Determine and describe any pollution control, treatment or pre-treatment equipment or operations (e.g., wastewater treatment or air pollution control

equipment) now or previously used at the property, including for each the purpose, flow or throughput rate, size, type, and age.

3. Determine the type, quantity and storage of fuels used at the property.

   a. Heating

   b. Vehicle

   c. Other

4. Determine any chemicals, compounds, or substances used in or stored at the property (name, hazard class, and volume per month).

5. Solid Wastes

   a. Determine and describe all wastes generated or handled at the property, the quantities of each, and how they were handled, stored, and disposed. For hazardous wastes, determine waste codes and obtain any available analyses and reports.

   b. Determine the wastes which are generated by air emission control systems at the property and the manner in which they are handled.

6. Wastewater Issues

   a. Determine the total annual process wastewater discharge and the place of discharge.

   b. Determine the total non-contact cooling water discharge and the place of discharge.

    c.   Determine the total sanitary wastewater discharge and the place of discharge.

    d.   Determine the total surface runoff water discharge, the place of discharge, and any treatment thereof.

    e.   Determine wastewater constituents which are monitored and the results of any monitoring.

    f.   Evaluate potential restrictions on wastewater discharges due to POTW capacity and/or water quality.

7. Air Issues

    a.   Determine whether any stationary sources of air pollutants discharge from the property.

    b.   Determine whether there is any equipment or process for which an air permit has been issued.

    c.   Evaluate whether the facility is located in an attainment or non- attainment area with respect to National Ambient Air Quality Standards, and whether potential facility expansions or modifications could be effected.

C. Indoor and Miscellaneous Environmental Issues

1. Asbestos

    a. If asbestos has ever been located on any part of the property, determine, if applicable, the removal process, the disposal process and whether federal and local regulations were followed, and obtain any available documentation.

    b. Determine the presence of any asbestos or asbestos containing materials at the property, and any on-going asbestos maintenance, abatement, and/or operations plan in effect.

    c. Evaluate compliance with state/governmental requirements concerning Asbestos, including requirements concerning record- keeping, warning signs, and training.

2. PCB's

    a. Determine any equipment containing PCBs on the property and any PCB spills or leaks.

    b. Determine PCB inspection, labeling and storage or management procedures, and provide documentation.

3. Radon

    a. Determine whether the property or any facility on the property has been tested for radon. If so, obtain results of the tests and reports as to any remediation system.

    b. Determine radon levels typically found in the vicinity of the property.

    c. If necessary, evaluate potential remedial action.

4. Lead

    a. Determine whether any water piping on the property contains lead (including lead-containing solder).

    b. Obtain any test results for drinking water.

    c. Determine whether paint on buildings, structures or equipment at the property contains lead.

    d. Determine any locations where paint on a structure, building or equipment is peeling.

5. Chlorofluorocarbons

    a. Determine the usage of chlorofluorocarbons at the property, including with respect to all systems serving buildings on the property. Consider impact of cost of replacement with systems which do not use chlorofluorocarbons.

6. Drinking Water

    a. Determine quality of drinking water and compliance with state and local laws

D.   Adjacent Properties.

  a. Determine adjacent land usage (developed, commercial, industrial, residential) at the property.

  b. Determine names of current adjacent landowners and the location of their properties, and to the degree possible, their financial viability.

  c. Determine previous uses of adjacent land.

  d. Determine and describe any waste disposal sites, landfills, pits, ponds or lagoons located within one-quarter mile of the property.

  e. Determine any state sites located within one mile of the property which are listed in a hazardous or any similar list.

  f. Determine whether any government agencies have required remediation or testing with respect to any location within one mile of the property.

  g. Determine whether runoff from adjacent sites flows onto the property or into surface water or storm drainage systems that serve the property.

  h. Determine area-wide groundwater flow conditions and direction.

E. Documentation to be Reviewed to Provide Information Concerning Subject Matters Set Forth Above

 1. From the Property Owner:

  a. regulatory notices and current and past permits, permit applications and regulatory agency files and correspondence.

  b. documents concerning past or present enforcement actions against the property resulting from non-compliance with environmental laws.

  c. responses to audit inquiry letters pertaining to the property.

  d. warning signs posted at the property, and information as to when they were first posted.

  e. warnings placed on any products produced at the property, and when the warning was first provided.

  f. material safety data sheets for materials produced or used at the property.

  g. reports or surveys with respect to any spill or other environmentally related incident.

h. spill-control plans which have been developed and implemented with respect to the property.

i. emergency response plans

j. maps and aerial photographs of the property (may need to be obtained from third-parties or government agencies)

k. notices from environmental groups, specifically including those prerequisite to filing of citizen suits to enforce federal, state, or other environmental laws and regulations.

l. spill reports and notifications, administrative complaints, compliance orders, injunctions, or other proceedings including compensatory and punitive assessments, fines, or penalties pursuant to any federal, state or other environmental statute or regulation.

m. environmental policies and procedures

n. waste manifests

o. discharge monitoring reports and other reports for any pollution discharge

p. environmental litigation files and administrative response files.

q. any previous Phase I or Phase II studies, or other environmental studies of the subject property, and if possible, adjacent properties.

r. groundwater and soil sampling and testing results.

s. environmental compliance audits performed internally or by outside personnel with respect to the operations of seller or previous owners or tenants at the property.

t. flood plain maps and available wetlands delineation maps (may need to get from third-parties)

u. for sellers that are public companies, any notification to the relevant stock exchange regarding material effects resulting from compliance with federal and state laws or regulations or pending or contemplated administrative or judicial proceedings arising under federal, state or local laws.

v. Financial documents relating to adjacent owners (will likely need to be obtained from third-parties)

EXHIBIT A

LENDER'S TITLE INSURANCE REQUIREMENTS CHECKLIST

PROPERTY:

CITY: [City]

STATE: [State]

ADDRESS: [Property Address]
COUNTY: [County]

PROPERTY NAME: [Common
name of Property]

TITLE COMPANY: Title Insurance
Company

TITLE COMMITMENT NO.:

BORROWER:

[Name of Borrowing Entity]

LENDER: _____

1.   <u>Title Insurance Company Requirements</u>:

    a.   The maximum single risk (i.e., the amount insured under any one policy) by a title insurer may not exceed 25% of that insurer's surplus and statutory reserves.

    b.   The Policy must be written by an insurer authorized to do business in the jurisdiction in which the Mortgaged Property is located.

2.   Loan Policy Forms.

3.   Insurance Amount. The amount insured must equal at least the original principal amount of the Loan.

4. <u>Named Insured</u>. The named insured under the Policy must be substantially the same as the following: "_____, and its successors and assigns."

5. <u>Creditors' Rights</u>. Any "creditors' rights" exception or other exclusion from coverage for voidable transactions under bankruptcy, fraudulent conveyance or other debtor protection laws or equitable principles must be removed by either an endorsement or a written waiver.

6. <u>Arbitration</u>. In the event that the form Policy which is utilized includes a compulsory arbitration provision, the insurer must agree that such compulsory arbitration provisions do not apply to any claims by or on behalf of the insured.

7. <u>Date of Policy</u>. The effective date of the Policy must be as of the date and time of the Closing, but, if a gap closing (i.e., a funding of the loan prior to the recording of the Mortgage) shall be authorized by _____and the Mortgage (or Deed of Trust - either of which are hereinafter referred to as a "Mortgage") shall not be recorded until after the Closing, upon the recording of the Mortgage the Policy shall be redated as of the date of the recording of the Mortgage.

8. <u>Legal Description</u>. The legal description of the Mortgaged Property contained in the Policy must conform to (i) the legal description shown on the survey of the Mortgaged Property, <u>and</u> (ii) the legal description contained in the Mortgage. In any event, the Policy must be endorsed to provide that the insured legal description is the same as that shown on the survey.

9.   <u>Easements</u>. Each Policy shall insure, as separate parcels: (a) all appurtenant easements and other estates benefiting the Mortgaged Property, and (b) all other rights, title and interests of the borrower in real property under reciprocal easement agreements, access agreements, operating agreements and agreements containing covenants, conditions and restrictions relating to the Mortgaged Property.

10. <u>Tax, Judgment and Lien Searches</u>. Tax, judgment and lien searches must be made no earlier than 30 days before the closing of the loan against the borrower and the indemnitors (identified as such in the Loan Commitment) in (i) the county where the Mortgaged Property is located, (ii) the governmental office (or other appropriate office) of the state where the Mortgaged Property is located, (iii) the county where any such party has its principal place of business or, if an individual, its residence, (iv) the governmental office (or other appropriate office) of the state where any such party has its principal place of business or, if an individual, its residence, and (v) if not already covered, the governmental office (or other appropriate office) of the states of formation of each of the foregoing entities.

11. <u>Exception to Coverage</u>. With respect to the exceptions, the following applies:

a.   Based upon representations made by the title insurer, each Policy shall afford the broadest coverage available in the state in which the Mortgaged Property is located. In addition, each Policy shall state that the

Mortgage is a valid first lien on the Mortgaged Property.

b. With respect to the "standard" exception (such as for parties in possession or other matters not shown on public records), such exceptions must be deleted.

c. With respect to the "standard" exception regarding tenants in possession under residential leases, such exception should also be deleted. In the alternative, the exception should read as follows: "Rights or claims of parties in possession under residential leases or occupants of apartment units, as tenants only."

d. The "standard" survey exception to the Policy must be deleted. Instead, a survey reading reflecting the current survey should be incorporated.

e. Any exception for taxes, assessments or other lienable items must expressly insure that such taxes, assessments or other items are not yet due and payable.

f. Any lien, encumbrance, covenant, condition, restriction or easement and other matters of record must be listed in the Policy and may remain if such exception would be acceptable to mortgage lending institutions generally or is covered by affirmative insurance generally acceptable to mortgage lending institutions. The Policy must affirmatively insure that the improvements do not encroach upon the listed easements or insure against all loss or damage due to such encroachment.

g. The Policy may not contain any exception for any filed or unfiled mechanics' or material men's liens.

h. In the event that a comprehensive endorsement has been issued and any Schedule B exceptions continue to be excluded from the coverage provided through that endorsement, then a determination must be made whether such exceptions would be acceptable to.

i. If Schedule B indicates the presence of any easements that are not located on the survey, the Policy must provide affirmative insurance against any loss resulting from the exercise by the holder of such easement of its right to use or maintain the easement.

12. Endorsements. With respect to endorsements, the following applies (unless by law such endorsements are not available in a particular jurisdiction):

a. Each Policy must include an acceptable environmental protection lien endorsement on the appropriate governmental form (if any).

b. Each Policy must contain an endorsement which provides that the insured legal description is the same as shown on the survey.

c. Each Policy must contain a comprehensive endorsement if a lien, encumbrance, condition, restriction or easement is listed in Schedule B to the title insurance policy.

d. The following endorsements shall be included in each Policy (unless inapplicable given the circumstances of the transaction):

- access
- zoning

- assignment of loan documents
- contiguity
- single tax lot
- doing business
- due execution
- mortgage tax
- usury
- address
- assignment of leases and rents
- assessments
- mineral rights
- reverter
- subdivision
- leasehold
- tie-in
- first loss
- last dollar

13. <u>Other Coverages</u>. Each Policy shall insure the following by endorsement or affirmative insurance.

    a.   that no conditions, covenants or restrictions of record affecting the Mortgaged Property:

- have been violated,

- create lien rights which prime the insured mortgage,

- contain a right of reverter or forfeiture, a right of reentry or power of termination, or

- if violated in the future would result in the lien created by the insured mortgage, or title to the Mortgaged Property being lost, forfeited or subordinated; and

b. that except for temporary interference resulting sole-ly from maintenance, repair, replacement or alteration of lines, facilities or equipment located in easements and rights of way taken as certain exceptions to each Policy, such exceptions do not and shall not prevent the use and operation of the Mortgaged Property or the improvements as used and operated on the effec-tive date of the Policy.

14. Informational Matters. The Policy must include, as an informational note, the following:

a. The recorded plat number together with recording in-formation; and

b. The property parcel number or the tax identification number, as applicable.

15. Financing Statements. Any financing statements filed or recorded showing the Lender as secured party must be shown as an informational note only. Such financing statements (and any assignments thereof) may not be listed as exceptions on Schedule B.

16. Delivery of Copies. All copies of all easements, encum-brances or other restrictions shown as exceptions on the Policy must be delivered.

EXHIBIT B

TO THE SURVEYOR

Please prepare three (3) original copies, signed and sealed by you, of a survey of the real property that is the subject of this transaction or financing meeting the specifications set forth herein. In connection with the preparation of the survey, you will be furnished with a recent title insurance commitment with respect to the real property and copies of all of the easements, rights-of-way and other title exceptions noted therein. The survey should be accompanied by three (3) copies of a consolidated perimeter metes and bounds description and, if required by the owner or the purchaser of the real property, the lender or the title insurer, three (3) copies of a surveyor's report in a specified form. The survey shall indicate the following:

1. The scale of the survey.

2. The North direction indicated by an arrow.

3. The beginning point definitively located in the dimensions of the Property.

4. The courses and distances (including radii and chords of all curved lines and their tangent points located by coordinates) of the entire perimeter. No distance shall be marked "more or less" except those that begin, terminate or bind on water or marshland, and in that event the limits of "more or less" must be set forth in feet.

5. The location and grades of all improvements on, as well as the physical characteristics of, the Property, such as walls, fences, streets, parking lots, buildings, driveways, visible utility installations to point of connection with any public system, cemeteries, streams and other water bodies, and all monuments and markers.

6. The meridian line drawn through one of the corners of the perimeter of the Property and another line drawn at right angles to said meridian through the same point. The meridian so drawn shall be either a true meridian or the magnetic meridian as of the date of the survey and so marked on the survey. All the courses and distances and coordinates shown on the survey shall be calculated from the said meridian and right angle line.

7. The width of any streets, alleys, curbs and pavements that abut or traverse the Property. The names of and distances to the nearest intersecting streets must be shown. The names of all dedicated public streets and alleys that abut or traverse the Property.

8. The total acreage of the Property in acres and in square feet.

9. Interior lines and facts sufficient to enable the title insurance company to insure contiguity if the Property comprises several parcels. All gaps, strips or gores must be shown with dimensions.

10. The location of any and all recorded easements or rights-of-way that are capable of being located (such as utility easements, set-backs, support easements,

party walls, easements and rights-of-way required by the municipal, county or state authorities, etc.) with each recording references shown on the survey. If any such easements or rights-of-way cannot be located, please so state on the survey, making reference to the applicable recording references. If any such easements or rights-of-way do not apply to the Property, please so state on the survey, making reference to the applicable recording references.

11. The location of any required set-back lines (whether by governmental requirement or recorded agreement) and the measured distance from the nearest edge of any building to the property line or public street.

12. The location of any tax lot lines or subdivision lot lines that (a) traverse the Property, or (b) include more land than the Property.

13. The zoning, use and density classification of the Property and the location of any lines that divide the Property into different classifications. The plat should designate the front yard lot line of the Property, as determined pursuant to applicable zoning regulations.

14. The location of the mean high and low water marks, or the mean height above sea level.

EXHIBIT C

[TO BE PLACED DIRECTLY ONTO SURVEY]

CERTIFICATION OF SURVEYOR

I,_____, hereby certify to [INSERT NAME OF BORROWER],

[INSERT NAME OF LENDER], [INSERT NAME OF TITLE INSURANCE COMPANY], and to all other parties interested in title to the property that is the subject of this survey (the "Property") that:

a. The survey prepared by me entitled "[INSERT TITLE OF SURVEY]" was actually made upon the ground and that it and the information, courses and distances shown thereon are correct;

b. The title lines and lines of actual possession are the same;

c. The size, location and type of buildings and improvements are as shown and all are within the boundary lines of the Property;

d. There are no uses, encroachments or easements either way across property lines affecting the Property appearing from a careful inspection of the same;

e. The Property consists of one or more complete lots of land complying with all applicable subdivision laws, rules and regulations;

f. The zoning of the Property is proper for the buildings and improvements existing thereon, and there are no violations of zoning ordinances, restrictions or other rules and regulations with respect to the location of said buildings and improvements;

g. All water, sewer, gas, electric and telephone lines and mains and all utility easements on the Property are located as shown on the survey;

h. All utility services required for the operation of the Property either enter the Property through adjoining public streets or the survey shows the point of entry and location of any utilities which pass through or are located on adjoining private land;

i. The survey shows the location and direction of all storm drain systems for the collection and disposal of all roof and surface drainage, and any discharge into streams, rivers and other conveyance systems;

j. I have reviewed Interim Title Insurance Commitment No. _____dated_____, 20____ issued by [INSERT NAME OF TITLE INSURANCE COMPANY], through its agent, [INSERT NAME OF TITLE INSURANCE AGENT], and have shown on the survey all of the exceptions contained in Schedule B of that commitment or, if any of such exceptions cannot be located, the same are indicated in the Notes appearing on this Survey;

[Manual signature of registered surveyor]_____

Date:_____, 20____

Please affix seal and note license number of registered surveyor.

This checklist was developed by Pytheas Limited and used with permission.